ENVIRONMENTAL
ISSUES

ENVIRONMENTAL DISASTERS

By Emilie Dufresne

KidHaven
PUBLISHING

Published in 2020 by
KidHaven Publishing, an Imprint of Greenhaven Publishing, LLC
353 3rd Avenue
Suite 255
New York, NY 10010

Edited by: Kristy Holmes
Designed by: Amy Li

Cataloging-in-Publication Data

Names: Dufresne, Emilie.
Title: Environmental disasters / Emilie Dufresne.
Description: New York : KidHaven Publishing, 2020. | Series: Environmental issues | Includes glossary and index.
Identifiers: ISBN 9781534530690 (pbk.) | ISBN 9781534530348 (library bound) | ISBN 9781534531666 (6 pack) | ISBN 9781534530652
(ebook)
Subjects: LCSH: Environmental disasters--Juvenile literature.
Classification: LCC GE146.D847 2020 | DDC 363.7'02--dc23

Printed in the United States of America

CPSIA compliance information: Batch #BS19KL: For further information contact Greenhaven Publishing LLC,
New York, New York at 1-844-317-7404.

Please visit our website, www.greenhavenpublishing.com. For a free color catalog of all our
high-quality books, call toll free 1-844-317-7404 or fax 1-844-317-7405.

Words that look like **this** can be found in the glossary on page 24.

Photo credits – Images are courtesy of Shutterstock.com. With thanks to Getty Images, Thinkstock Photo and iStockphoto.
Cover – Buffy1982, Thanakrit Homsiri, 1 – IhorL, 2 – fboudrias, 3 – IrinaK, 4 – austinding, 5 – Chris Warham, 6 – Doug McLean,
7 – sandyman, 8 – leungchopan, 9 – Tigergallery, 10 – Mike Shooter, 11 – David Bailey, 12 – Fotokostic, 13 – vesilvio, 14 – Byelikova
Oksana, 15 – Chukov, 16 – Anjo Kan, 17 – Patrick K. Campbell, 18 – Patrik Mezirka, 19 – Greg Hume (wikipedia), 20 – Giedriius,
21 – vasakkohaline, 22 – Forrest Dix, Kaspri, 23 – Martin Lisner.

CONTENTS

WHAT IS A DISASTER?

A disaster is a sudden event that causes a lot of damage to the **environment** and human life. Disasters are very dangerous events that cause many problems.

Big disasters can be very expensive to fix. This can make the effects of the disaster last longer. This is because people may not be able to afford the time, money, and helpers needed to recover.

CHARITIES OFTEN COME AND GIVE FOOD, WATER, AND MEDICAL AID TO VICTIMS OF DISASTER.

TYPES OF DISASTERS

There are two types of disasters: natural and environmental.

Natural disasters are disasters that happen because of natural causes. Some examples of natural disasters are earthquakes, floods, and volcanic eruptions.

Environmental disasters are disasters that happen because of human actions. Some examples of environmental disasters are oil spills, chemical explosions, and gas leaks.

LET'S LOOK AT SOME DIFFERENT KINDS OF ENVIRONMENTAL DISASTERS.

INDUSTRIAL DISASTERS

The word "industry" means the factories, machines, and processes that are used to create different products.

ANY DISASTER THAT IS RELATED TO INDUSTRY IS KNOWN AS AN INDUSTRIAL DISASTER.

OIL SPILLS HAPPEN WHEN SHIPS LEAK THE OIL THEY ARE CARRYING.

Industrial disasters include nuclear explosions, gas leaks, and oil spills. These disasters are often accidents, or happen because **equipment** isn't looked after properly.

Industrial disasters can cause a lot of damage to plants, animals, and people. Oil doesn't mix with water, so when an oil spill happens, the oil floats on top of the water.

THE OIL IS VERY HARD TO CLEAN UP AS IT STICKS TO WHATEVER IT TOUCHES, LIKE THIS BIRD.

IT CAN BE
HARD FOR PLANTS AND
ANIMALS TO SURVIVE IN
AREAS WHERE INDUSTRIAL
DISASTERS HAPPEN.

Oil spills, gas leaks, and nuclear explosions release dangerous materials into the environment. This can **contaminate** the area with **hazardous** materials.

AGRICULTURAL DISASTERS

The word "agriculture" refers to the machinery, fields, animals, and plants that are used to help us produce food.

THERE ARE LOTS OF DIFFERENT KINDS OF AGRICULTURAL DISASTERS.

Agricultural disasters can be caused by watering an area too little or too much, plowing the land too much, or overusing **pesticides**.

THESE CAN ALL CAUSE SERIOUS PROBLEMS FOR THE ENVIRONMENT.

Some pesticides are dangerous to humans and animals. They can build up in the soil, making it harder for the crops to grow. Plowing and watering too little or too much can also make the land **barren**.

It takes a long time for the soil to get back all the **nutrients** it loses from being watered, plowed, and sprayed with pesticides.

BIODIVERSITY DISASTERS

Biodiversity means having many different types of animals and plants in one area. Having good biodiversity is better for the **ecosystem**.

CANE TOADS WERE INTRODUCED TO AUSTRALIA TO CONTROL PESTS.

Biodiversity disasters often happen when humans introduce a new animal or plant to an area that they don't normally live in. This is often done to control a **native species**.

Introduced species often eat the food and take the homes of native species. This might make it hard for the native species to survive there.

GRAY SQUIRRELS WERE INTRODUCED TO THE UK IN THE 1870s. THEY TAKE A LOT OF FOOD AND SHELTER THAT THE NATIVE RED SQUIRRELS THERE NEED.

This ko'ko' bird is now **endangered** because the brown tree snake was introduced to its environment. Like many introduced species, the snake has no **predators** and is quickly growing in number.

AFTER AN ENVIRONMENTAL DISASTER

Environmental disasters have long-lasting effects on the planet. For example, plant and animal life might never adjust to an introduced species after a biodiversity disaster.

RED SQUIRREL NUMBERS ARE STILL FALLING SINCE GRAY SQUIRRELS WERE INTRODUCED.

SITE OF NUCLEAR EXPLOSION

CAUTION

RADIOACTIVE MATERIALS

After an industrial disaster, dangerous chemicals can be found in the area for years and years afterward. These areas can become so dangerous that humans can no longer visit them.

ENVIRONMENTAL DISASTER FACTS

One way to get rid of oil on the sea is to burn it. This does get rid of the oil, but it also releases harmful gases into the environment.

An area in Ukraine where a nuclear disaster happened in 1986 could be contaminated with radiation for around 300 years.

Of all endangered species, 42 percent are at risk because of introduced animals and plants.

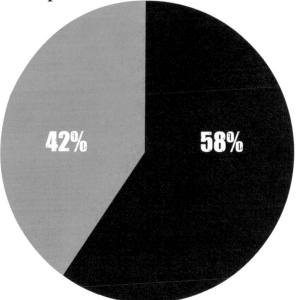

42% 58%

AT RISK FROM INTRODUCED SPECIES

OTHER RISKS

ENDANGERED SPECIES

If there are dangerous chemicals in an area, people might have to wear **hazmat suits**. These keep people from becoming ill from the chemicals.

GLOSSARY

barren   not able to produce or support the growth of crops

contaminate   to make something unclean by adding a harmful substance to it

ecosystem   a community of living things and the environment in which they live

endangered   when a species of animal is in danger of going extinct

environment   the natural world

equipment   items that are needed to complete a certain job

hazardous   something that has great risk or danger

hazmat suits   full-body suits that protect people

native species   an animal or plant that originally came from a particular environment or ecosystem

nutrients   natural substances that plants and animals need to grow and stay healthy

pesticides   chemicals used to kill animals and insects that damage crops

predators   animals that hunt other animals for food

INDEX